REVIEW COPY
COURTESY OF
COMPASS POINT BOOKS

D1604897

WE THE PEOPLE

Vietnam Veterans Memorial

by Natalie M. Rosinsky

Content Adviser: Marc Leepson,
Vietnam Veterans of America,
Silver Spring, Maryland

Reading Adviser: Rosemary G. Palmer, Ph.D.,
Department of Literacy, College of Education
Boise State University

COMPASS POINT BOOKS

MINNEAPOLIS, MINNESOTA

Compass Point Books
3109 West 50th Street, #115
Minneapolis, MN 55410

Visit Compass Point Books on the Internet at *www.compasspointbooks.com*
or e-mail your request to *custserv@compasspointbooks.com*

On the cover: Detail of inscribed names from the Vietnam Veterans Memorial Wall in
Washington, D.C.

Photographs ©: James P. Blair/Corbis, cover, 22; Library of Congress, back cover; Prints Old and
Rare, back cover (far left); Wally McNamee/Corbis, 4, 6, 34; Bettmann/Corbis, 7, 9, 10, 11, 12, 13,
16, 20, 24, 26; Charles Bonnay/Time Life Pictures/Getty Images, 8; JP Laffont/Sygma/Corbis, 15;
United Artists/Getty Images, 17; Todd Gipstein/Corbis, 19, 21; David Hume Kennerly/Getty Images,
27; William Manning/Corbis, 28; Ron Sachs/CNP/Corbis, 30; Gregg Newton/Corbis, 31; Pablo
Cuarterolo/AFP/Getty Images, 32; Svetlana Zhurkin, 35; AP/Wide World Photos/Wilfredo Lee, 36;
Joe Raedle/Getty Images, 39; Steve Raymer/Corbis, 40.

Managing Editor: Catherine Neitge
Page Production: Heather Griffin
Photo Researcher: Marcie C. Spence
Cartographer: XNR Productions, Inc.
Library Consultant: Kathleen Baxter

Creative Director: Keith Griffin
Editorial Director: Carol Jones

Library of Congress Cataloging-in-Publication Data
Rosinsky, Natalie M. (Natalie Myra)
 Vietnam Veterans Memorial / by Natalie M. Rosinsky.
      p. cm.
 Includes bibliographical references and index.
  ISBN-13: 978-0-7565-2032-8 (hardcover)
  ISBN-10: 0-7565-2032-0 (hardcover)
  ISBN-13: 978-0-7565-2044-1 (paperback)
  ISBN-10: 0-7565-2044-4 (paperback)
  1. Vietnam Veterans Memorial (Washington, D.C.)—Juvenile literature. I. Title. II. We the people
(Series) (Compass Point Books)
  DS559.83.W18.R66 2006
  959.704'36—dc22   2006003945

TABLE OF CONTENTS

A TIME OF HEALING

Tears trailed down some faces. Others held proud smiles beneath eyes shadowed by memories. Strong feelings brought these 150,000 people to Washington, D.C., on Veterans Day, November 13, 1982. They were watching the dedication of a new national monument, the Vietnam

Veterans and their families mobbed the memorial at its dedication.

Veterans Memorial. The Vietnam War had touched their lives in unforgettable ways. Some had fought in Vietnam. Others lost friends and loved ones in the conflict. Some in the huge crowd had opposed the war. As part of the dedication ceremony, Navy chaplain Arnold E. Resnicoff prayed that this day would be a "time of healing" for the entire country.

After an hour of speeches and the singing of "God Bless America," veteran leader Jan C. Scruggs announced, "Ladies and gentlemen, the Vietnam Veterans Memorial is now dedicated." Thousands of people pushed forward, crushing fences that had been erected to manage the enormous gathering. Hands reached out to touch the monument. The long, black wall was engraved with the names of 57,939 American servicemen and servicewomen killed or missing in Vietnam. One emotional veteran even climbed to the top of the wall and played his bugle. Far into the night, people waited for their chance to touch the names of lost friends and relatives.

*Veterans paraded to the memorial
before its dedication.*

Before the dedication, thousands had paraded down Constitution Avenue toward the monument, which is known to many as the Wall. Members of marching bands wore bright, shiny uniforms. So did some veterans. Others dressed in the worn, brown and green clothing they had used in battle. Some wounded veterans rolled slowly down the avenue in wheelchairs. One man carried a handmade sign that read, "I am a Vietnam Veteran. I like the memorial. And if it makes it difficult to send people into battle again, I like it even more." His sign was a response to earlier, heated disagreements about this particular monument. The monument's design was controversial, just as the Vietnam War had been.

A War Both Far and Near

Vietnam is a small country about the size of New Mexico located in Southeast Asia. Few Americans had traveled to distant Vietnam until the 1950s. That is when the Vietnamese people won their independence from France.

French prisoners of war marched from battle in 1954 when France lost control of Vietnam.

7

Ho Chi Minh (1890–1969)

This European nation had ruled Vietnam as a colony for nearly 100 years.

Vietnam was divided into two countries, North Vietnam and South Vietnam. In 1954, the two new countries were at odds. Leader Ho Chi Minh of North Vietnam supported communism, a system in which goods and property are owned by the government and shared in common. The leader of South Vietnam, Ngo Dinh Diem, supported democracy, a form of government in which the people elect their leaders. Even though Ho Chi Minh was popular in both countries and some people believed Ngo Dinh Diem was dishonest, the U.S. government began to side with South Vietnam.

American officials did not want another communist

Ngo Dinh Diem took the oath of office as president of South Vietnam in 1955.

country in the world. Most Americans believed that communism threatened to destroy democracy. U.S. leaders feared that if Vietnam united under communism, other

9

General William Westmoreland, commander of U.S. troops, used a map of Vietnam to make a point.

countries nearby would soon become communist, too. They called this fear the domino theory. They compared the countries in the area to a row of standing dominoes. Vietnam was seen as the first falling domino, which would immediately cause the rest of them to fall.

The United States began to send military advisers to South Vietnam. Then in 1959, the first Americans were killed in the struggle between North and South Vietnamese forces. It was not until the 1960s, however, that large numbers of U.S. troops entered the conflict. In 1965, President Lyndon B. Johnson began increasing America's military presence in Vietnam. By 1966, nearly

10

Members of the Army's 101st Airborne Division waded across a river during the war.

200,000 Americans were fighting in Vietnam. By 1967, U.S. forces there had more than doubled, to nearly 500,000.

Even though battles were fought far away from the United States, photographs and TV news broadcasts brought daily pictures of the war's bloodshed and terror. To many Americans, the Vietnam War was as nearby as the closest television set or newspaper.

HAWKS AND DOVES

Some Americans believed strongly in U.S. efforts in Vietnam. They wanted more troops and weapons sent there until the communists were defeated. As aggressive as birds of prey, these war supporters were called hawks.

A helicopter picked up supplies in South Vietnam.

12

Some hawks felt it was their patriotic duty to support American soldiers no matter where they fought.

Other Americans did not support U.S. involvement in the Vietnam War. They noted that some South Vietnamese people themselves respected Ho Chi Minh and his communist ideas. These Americans were called doves, because this gentle bird is often a symbol of peace.

Many doves did not believe in the domino theory

Battle-weary soldiers paused for a moment after a bloody battle in 1967.

about the spread of communism. They did not think that young American men should be required to fight in Vietnam. The U.S. government policy known as the draft required young men to serve in the military. It was used more and more during the Vietnam War since there were not enough volunteers to serve in the military. Many of the young men who fought in Vietnam went there because they had to. They had no choice.

Doves began to protest the war. They held large antiwar demonstrations and marches, including demonstrations in Washington, D.C. On October 15, 1969, about 250,000 people attended an antiwar demonstration there. On the same day, an estimated 2 million people were attending similar peace rallies and meetings throughout the United States. Sometimes, hawks showed up at these events to protest the antiwar activities.

In 1969, the United States began to withdraw troops from Vietnam. Because of the controversy about the war, though, returning soldiers were not always warmly

Washington, D.C., was the focal point of the 1969 nationwide Peace Moratorium.

welcomed home. Sometimes, veterans were even met by
protesters who called them murderers.

In 1973, the U.S. government agreed to a cease-fire
with North Vietnam. The last American combat troops
left Vietnam that year. The last American soldiers to die in
Vietnam were killed in 1975, as they defended U.S. civilians
and allies fleeing the country now united under communism.

Three soldiers helped each other to an evacuation helicopter after a fierce battle.

The United States did not win the war in Vietnam. After the cease-fire, no victory parades were held for returning troops. Yet, in addition to the millions of Vietnamese who lost their lives in the war, more than 58,000 Americans had died. And more than 300,000 were wounded in Vietnam. Of those injured, more than 6,000 lost an arm or leg and more than 33,000 were paralyzed. The end of the war did not end the pain and grief of the more than 2.5 million veterans, their families, and friends.

THE PRICE OF WAR

Maryland teenager Jan C. Scruggs had joined the Army
and was sent to Vietnam in 1969. He was wounded and
received a medal for bravery. Back in the United States,
Scruggs attended college, married, and got a job.

Scruggs lived quietly with his war memories until
1979, when he saw a powerful movie about the Vietnam

War called *The
Deer Hunter.* As
he later said,
the Academy
Award-winning
film made him
think of battles
and his "buddies
dead … their
brains and intes-
tines all over the

Michael Cimino directed Robert DeNiro in The Deer Hunter.

place." Scruggs became convinced that Americans needed to "feel the price of war … [to] understand that the price has to be paid in human lives."

Scruggs believed that a memorial to Vietnam veterans in the nation's capital would achieve this goal. He wanted the memorial to contain the name of every American who died in the war. Scruggs believed such a "sea of names" would both honor the dead and give his "generation of veterans their long-denied dignity."

Scruggs wanted a spot on the 2-mile-long (3-kilometer) National Mall to be the site of the memorial. He knew, however, that other memorials on the Mall, such as the Lincoln Memorial and the Washington Monument, had taken years to be approved and built. Scruggs would not accept such delays. He also did not aim for a war memorial paid for by the government. His vision was of a veterans memorial built with contributions from ordinary citizens.

Two other Vietnam veterans, Robert Doubek and John Wheeler, joined Scruggs in his efforts. These two

The memorial's "sea of names" honors those who died and are missing in Vietnam.

Washington lawyers and Scruggs formed a volunteer organization called the Vietnam Veterans Memorial Fund in 1979. They aimed to construct and dedicate a memorial by Veterans Day 1982. The men used their knowledge of politics and business to raise funds nationally and to meet an extraordinarily fast schedule. By 1980, they had convinced Congress to set aside land on the grassy National Mall for

19

1975

Jan C. Scruggs was the guiding force behind the Vietnam Veterans Memorial.

their monument. It would be next to the Lincoln Memorial.

The organization's leaders planned to complete fund-raising and select a design for the memorial in 1981. They did not realize that a new controversy would soon threaten their schedule.

20

Messages for All

More than 275,000 Americans contributed more than $7 million for the veterans memorial. Now, memorial fund leaders had to choose a design for the monument. They held an open competition, explaining their goals for the best design, and asked eight art experts to decide the winner. The memorial had to contain the names of

The memorial contains the names of the dead and missing in Vietnam in order by year.

all dead and missing Americans in Vietnam. It had to fit the landscape of the Mall and make people think. Yet, as Robert Doubek wrote, they did not want the memorial to make a "political statement about the war or its conduct. … The hope is that … the memorial will begin a healing process."

A V-shaped wall of black granite contains the names of the dead and missing.

The competition began in October 1980. Sculptors, architects, and others submitted 1,421 designs. The judges studied these designs carefully before declaring Entry 1,026 the winner. In their admiring words, "This is very much a memorial of our own times … an eloquent place where the simple meeting of earth, sky, and remembered names contains messages for all who will know this place."

The winning design was a V-shaped wall about 493 feet (150 meters) long. It was made up of separate panels of black granite, ranging in height from 8 inches (20 centimeters) to more than 10 feet (3 m). The names of the dead and missing were engraved on the panels in order by the date on which they had been lost.

To everyone's surprise, the creator of the winning design was a 21-year-old student. Maya Ying Lin was studying to be an architect at Yale University. Her vision for the memorial began as a homework assignment for one of her classes.

To plan her design, Lin had traveled to Washington.

23

Watching people play on the grassy mall inspired her. She later said, "I didn't want to destroy a living park. … I knew I wanted something horizontal that took you in, that made you feel safe within the park, yet at the same time reminding you of the dead." She began to think "about what death is, what a loss is. A sharp pain that lessens with time, but can never quite heal over. A scar." She imagined that if she took "a knife and cut open the earth … with

Jan Scruggs (left) and Robert Doubek display Maya Lin's winning design in 1981.

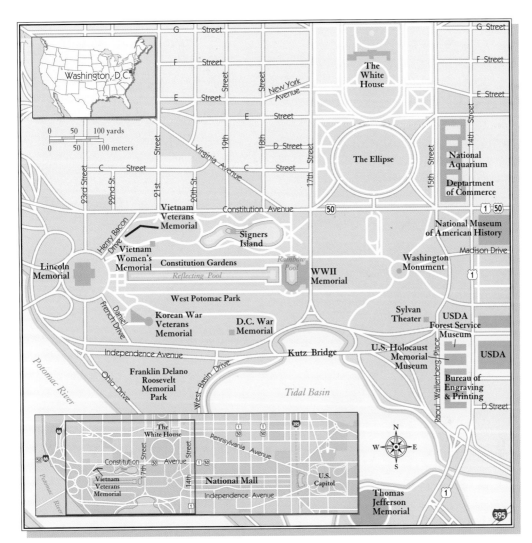

The Vietnam Veterans Memorial is next to the Lincoln Memorial on the Mall.

time the grass would heal it." Lin designed the memorial

so that such healing grass would grow close to its

black panels.

Vietnam veterans took a preview look at the memorial a few days before it was dedicated.

Lin's design caused controversy. One veteran called it an ugly "black gash of shame." He and others wanted a monument that showed the pain and courage of American soldiers in Vietnam. Some people wanted a white monument. Others disliked how Lin's design would make people walk downward to see some names. Lin explained that black is a soothing color. In bright sunlight, names would be easier to read on a black monument than on a white one. Lin thought it would be healing for visitors to the memorial to "have to walk back up into the light … to go beyond" death and loss.

Arguments went on for months. Secretary of the Interior James Watt for a time refused to permit the monument to be built because of the controversy. People for and

President Ronald Reagan (left) and Interior Secretary James Watt answered questions in 1982.

27

against the proposed memorial finally agreed on two additions to it. One would be a flagpole flying the American flag. The other was a 7-foot-tall (2-m), detailed, bronze statue of three American soldiers. They are young, stand close together, and wear the battle clothes and carry the weapons used in Vietnam. The sculptor of these figures,

The Three Fightingmen *statue stands near the Wall.*

28

Frederick Hart, explained that the "contrast between …

their youth and the weapons of war [points out] their sacri-

fice." Their closeness shows the love and trust that the

soldiers have come to share.

Even though *The Three Fightingmen* statue would

not be finished by the memorial's planned dedication date,

Watt approved the new monument. Ground was broken

for the Vietnam Veterans Memorial in March 1982. At

the ceremony, representatives from every state and veter-

ans organization showed their support by digging into the

earth. The memorial would be completed on time.

During the November 1982 dedication of the memo-

rial, Frederick Hart displayed a model of *The Three*

Fightingmen. The statue itself was placed on the Mall in

1984. From their nearby position, the young soldiers appear

to look toward the Wall carrying the names of their

lost comrades.

So Many Stories

Since its dedication, the Vietnam Veterans Memorial has become one of the most visited monuments in Washington, D.C. Between 20 million and 25 million people have stopped there to see or touch it. Many visitors bring items to leave at the Wall below the name of a lost friend or relative. About one-third of these items are military. They include medals and parts of uniforms belonging to the veterans or visitors.

Boots with a message were left at the Wall.

Another one-third are letters or cards written to the dead. One mother wrote to her son, "I miss you so much and

A man grieved during a Memorial Day visit to the Wall.

the hurt never ends. You are still with us in our hearts and

always will be. … Love, Mom." One veteran left a message

for his dead comrade. He wrote, "We did what we could

Two children made a rubbing of the engraved name of a loved one.

but it was not enough because I found you here. You are not just a name on this wall. You are alive. … I will never forget your face."

Other items left at the Wall hold special meaning

that strangers may not fully understand. Toys, books, teddy bears, and tennis rackets have been left there. National Park Service workers collect the items and store them in a special building in Maryland. As one caretaker said with respect, "These materials make up a very important part of the story of the Vietnam War. … So many stories are in them, so much feeling, emotion, heartache." In 1992, the Smithsonian's National Museum of American History in Washington, D.C., held the first exhibit of offerings left at the Wall. Since then, other museums around the country have also displayed some of the items.

Some visitors to the memorial take away a special souvenir. They make a rubbing of the engraved name or names they have come to see and touch.

FINALLY WELCOMED HOME

After the 1982 dedication of the memorial, Jan Scruggs said that "America's Vietnam veterans were finally welcomed home." In 1993, this welcome was extended to the estimated 15,000 women who served in Vietnam during the war. Military nurses and workers, news reporters, and Red Cross volunteers were honored with their own monument.

Female veterans attended the dedication of the Vietnam Women's Memorial.

34

A bronze statue near the Wall honors the women who served in Vietnam.

On Veterans Day 1993, the Vietnam Women's
Memorial was dedicated on the National Mall. It is a
bronze statue with four figures. A nurse supports a wounded
soldier, while another woman sits behind them with her
head bowed. A third woman looks upward, toward the sky
and possible rescue. Glenna Goodacre, who sculpted the
women's memorial, has said that she wanted to show the

July 4 fireworks lit up the Wall and the Washington Monument in the distance.

women's "emotions … their fatigue, and above all, their dedication." The statue is located just a short distance, about 100 yards (91 m), from the Wall.

Many visitors travel to the veterans memorials year-round. On Veterans Day, Memorial Day, Father's Day, and Mother's Day, special ceremonies take place at the Vietnam Veterans Memorial. The Wall is always lit at night and is staffed daily from 8 A.M. to midnight with National Park Service workers. Four sheltered areas also contain printed guides that indicate where names are located on the Wall. In 2003, President George W. Bush approved the construction of an underground education center for visitors to the Vietnam Veterans Memorial.

As veterans die from wounds suffered long ago in Vietnam, names continue to be added to the memorial. As of 2006, the Wall listed 58,249 veterans.

ACROSS THE COUNTRY
AND THE WORLD

Visiting the Vietnam Veterans Memorial is an emotional experience. Veteran John Wheeler said, "We begin to see hurts inside us, too, when we see our own reflections in the walls." Standing on the National Mall, visitors also can appreciate the full impact of what is now called the triangle of Vietnam veterans' memorials. The statue of *The Three Fightingmen* and the Vietnam Women's Memorial are just a turn of the head and a few steps away from the Wall.

It is now possible to share part of this experience without traveling to Washington, D.C. In 1996, the Vietnam Veterans Memorial Fund completed its project to have a half-size model of Maya Lin's Wall built. It is designed to travel to communities throughout the United States. Called "The Wall That Heals," the model also has a museum and information center that accompany it aboard a special bus. "The Wall That Heals" has traveled by

38

A New Mexico veteran cried as he found the name of a friend who died in Vietnam.

invitation to more than 250 communities across the country. In 1999, it was invited to Ireland, where Irish-Americans who served in Vietnam were honored.

The Wall is a source of comfort for veterans who lost friends in the war.

In 1998, the Internet began to provide another way for people around the world to experience the Vietnam Veterans Memorial. The Veterans Memorial Fund operates a Web site called The Virtual Wall. Online visitors can see and hear messages left by families, friends, and veterans themselves. Visitors can post their own messages at the virtual wall. It is even possible to make a virtual rubbing of one or more names displayed on the Web site's wall.

People continue to learn about and honor the sacrifices made during the Vietnam War and similar conflicts. The Vietnam Veterans Memorial acts as a source of healing, information, and inspiration for many in this process.

GLOSSARY

architects—people who design buildings and monuments

cease-fire—an end to battle without either side being declared the winner

chaplain—a member of the clergy attached to a branch of the military

controversy—a strong disagreement that receives public attention and causes public debate

eloquent—communicating ideas and feelings powerfully and convincingly

landscape—the natural state or landforms of an area

paralyzed—unable to move

rubbing—a method of tracing a word or image that has been engraved on stone

virtual—existing without physical limits, often used to refer to information on the Internet

DID YOU KNOW?

- In 1988, a TV movie was made about Jan C. Scruggs and his efforts to build the Vietnam Veterans Memorial. It is called *To Heal a Nation,* and it is based on the book Scruggs wrote.

- Other ideas submitted in the competition to design the Vietnam Veterans Memorial included plans for a 40-foot-tall (12-m) rocking chair and a two-story-high combat boot.

- The movie *Maya Lin: A Strong Clear Vision* won the 1995 Academy Award for best documentary film.

- Since designing the Vietnam Veterans Memorial, Lin has designed an outdoor peace chapel and monuments honoring the civil rights movement and women's education.

- Names on the wall are engraved in letters about one-half inch (1 cm) high. A diamond appears next to the names of those killed. A cross appears next to the names of those missing when the war ended.

- All states and many localities have their own monuments for their veterans killed or missing in Vietnam.

IMPORTANT DATES

Timeline

1965	First wave of U.S. combat troops arrives in Vietnam.
1967	About 500,000 U.S. troops are in Vietnam; large demonstrations and marches against the war begin in the United States.
1973	Cease-fire declared, and most U.S. troops leave Vietnam.
1979	Jan Scruggs begins efforts for the memorial.
1982	Memorial designed by Maya Ying Lin is completed and dedicated.
1984	*The Three Fightingmen* statue is set in place as part of the memorial.
1993	Vietnam Women's Memorial is erected.
1996	"The Wall That Heals" traveling exhibit is launched.
1998	The Virtual Wall Web site is established.
2003	President George W. Bush authorizes the planning and building of an underground education center at the Wall.

IMPORTANT PEOPLE

GLENNA GOODACRE (1940–)

Sculptor of the Vietnam Women's Memorial; a graduate of Colorado College, she is also the designer of the Sacagawea dollar coin that began circulating in 2000

FREDERICK HART (1943–1999)

Sculptor who designed The Three Fightingmen *statue, which is also known as* The Three Servicemen *and* The Three Soldiers; *Hart was an apprentice stone carver at the National Cathedral in Washington, D.C., working on gargoyles when he won an international competition to produce a huge sculpture for the cathedral; he died of lung cancer at age 55*

MAYA YING LIN (1959–)

American architect who designed the Vietnam Veterans Memorial while an undergraduate at Yale University; her parents fled China in 1949 when Mao Tse-tung came to power

JAN C. SCRUGGS (1950–)

Vietnam War veteran whose efforts led to the creation of the Vietnam Veterans Memorial; he grew up in Maryland and received his law degree from the University of Maryland, Baltimore

WANT TO KNOW MORE?

At the Library

Dunn, John M. *The Vietnam War: A History of U.S. Involvement.* San Diego: Lucent Books, 2001.

Kent, Deborah. *The Vietnam Women's Memorial.* Chicago: Childrens Press, 1995.

Malone, Mary. *Maya Lin: Architect and Artist.* Springfield, N.J.: Enslow Publishers, 1995.

McCormick, Anita Louise. *The Vietnam Antiwar Movement in American History.* Springfield, N.J.: Enslow Publishers, 2000.

Willis, Terri. *Vietnam.* New York: Children's Press, 2002.

Zeinert, Karen. *The Valiant Women of the Vietnam War.* Brookfield, Conn.: Millbrook Press, 2000.

On the Web

For more information on the *Vietnam Veterans Memorial,* use FactHound to track down Web sites related to this book.

1. Go to *www.facthound.com*

2. Type in a search word related to this book or this book ID: 0756520320

3. Click on the *Fetch It* button.

Your trusty FactHound will fetch the best Web sites for you!

On the Road

Vietnam Veterans Memorial

Bacon Drive and Constitution
Avenue on the National Mall
Washington, DC
202/426-6841
The Wall, *The Three Fightingmen,*
and the Vietnam Women's Memorial

The Wall That Heals

Vietnam Veterans Memorial Fund
202/393-0090
A half-scale replica of the Vietnam
Veterans Memorial that travels
to communities throughout the
United States

Look for more We the People books about this era:

The 19th Amendment
ISBN 0-7565-1260-3

The Berlin Airlift
ISBN 0-7565-2024-X

The Dust Bowl
ISBN 0-7565-0837-1

Ellis Island
ISBN 0-7565-0302-7

The Great Depression
ISBN 0-7565-0152-0

The Korean War
ISBN 0-7565-2027-4

Navajo Code Talkers
ISBN 0-7565-0611-5

Pearl Harbor
ISBN 0-7565-0680-8

The Persian Gulf War
ISBN 0-7565-0612-3

September 11
ISBN 0-7565-2029-0

The Sinking of the USS Indianapolis
ISBN 0-7565-2031-2

The Statue of Liberty
ISBN 0-7565-0100-8

The Titanic
ISBN 0-7565-0614-X

The Tuskegee Airmen
ISBN 0-7565-0683-2

A complete list of We the People titles is available on our Web site:
www.compasspointbooks.com

INDEX

About the Author

Natalie M. Rosinsky is the award-winning author of more than 90 publications. She writes about science, history, economics, social studies, and popular culture. One of her two cats usually sits near her computer as she works in Mankato, Minnesota. Natalie earned graduate degrees from the University of Wisconsin and has been a high school teacher and college professor as well as a corporate trainer.